CASIO

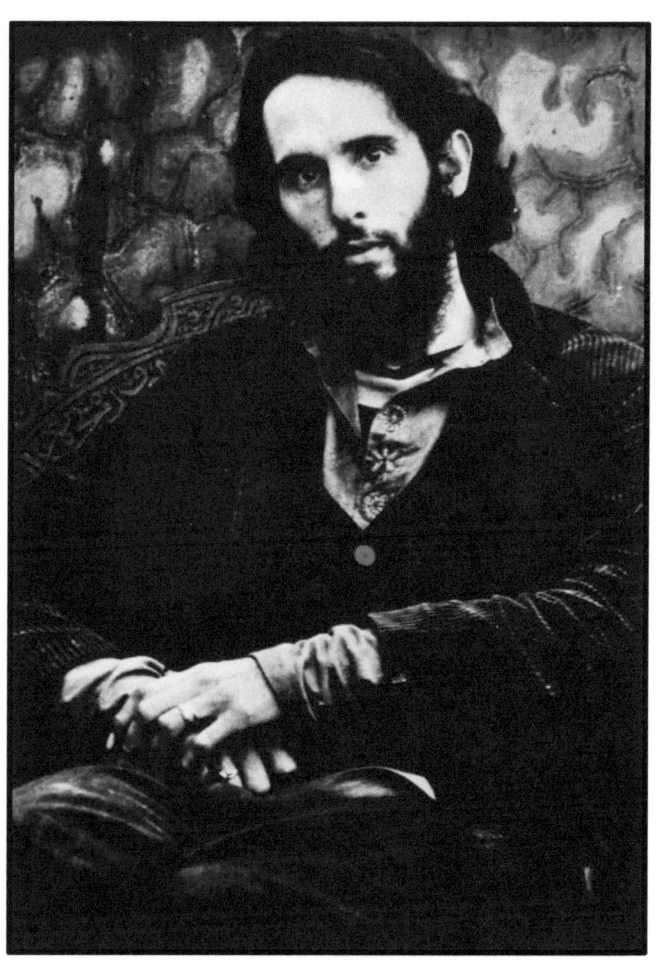

by Susanna Deiss

CASIO. Format and text copyright © 2017 by Susanna Deiss. All rights reserved. No part of this book may be used or reproduced in any manner whatsoever without written permission.

ISBN-13: 978-1977849830
ISBN-10: 1977849830

Published 2017 by *Panicale Press*.
For information address *Panicale Press:*
www.panicalepress.com
info@panicalepress.com

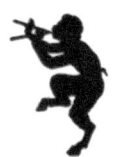

In Memory of my brother,
John Casy Deiss

Casio, 1940 – 1969

For his daughter,
I-La Casy Deiss

For a long time after my brother died I pretended that he was just off on another road trip, riding his motorcycle down back roads in Spain, or perhaps Morocco. It was a very long trip, and after 26 years I finally realized that Casio wasn't coming back.

I adored Casio, and trusted him. Once he rescued me when I fell through ice on our pond, risking his own life. But a sister has a different view from the rest of the world. I knew him long and well, and like everyone else, he wasn't perfect. I remember him teasing me, describing monsters when I was still so small that I was clinging to the railing of my crib as I howled.

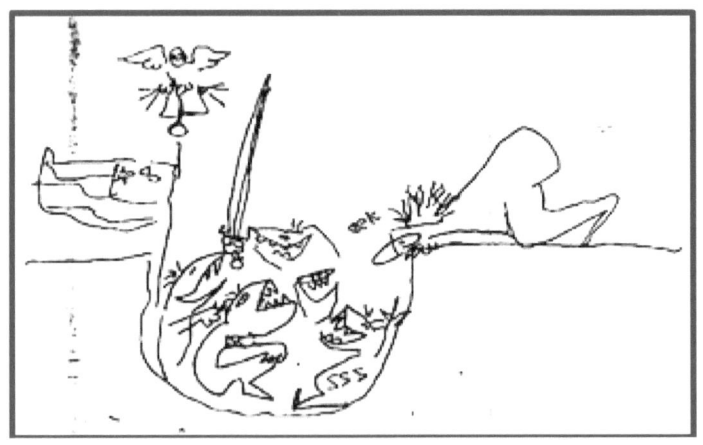

Monsters

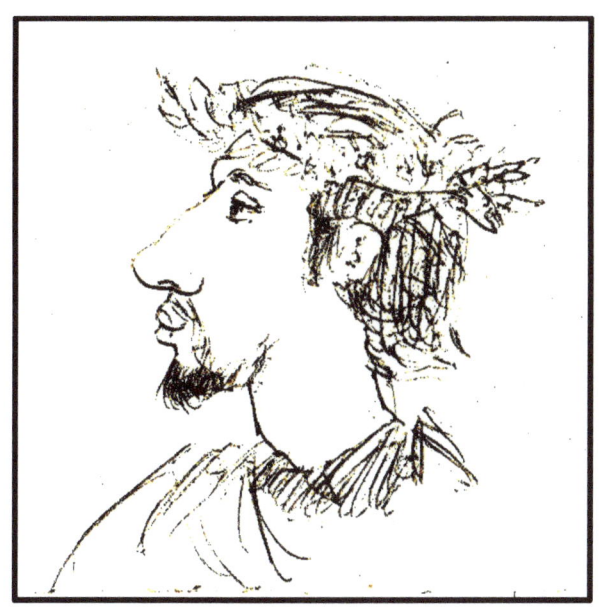

Self-Portrait

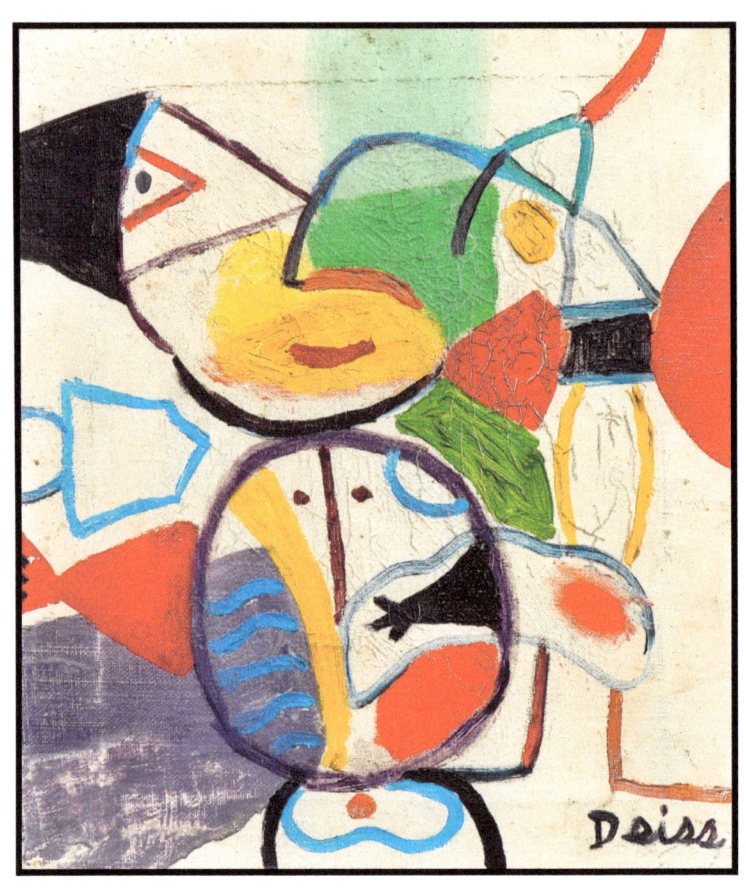

Tummy Touching

In the mid-1940s, our family was living in the Village in New York. We had an Irish Catholic nanny who terrified my brother with tales of hellfire if he touched himself. He insisted on wearing his underwear to bed at night, until our mild-mannered mother realized what was frightening him.

Mother dismissed the girl in a fury. When she was very angry, Mother would half close her eyes and sway. We rarely saw her angry, but this was one of those times.

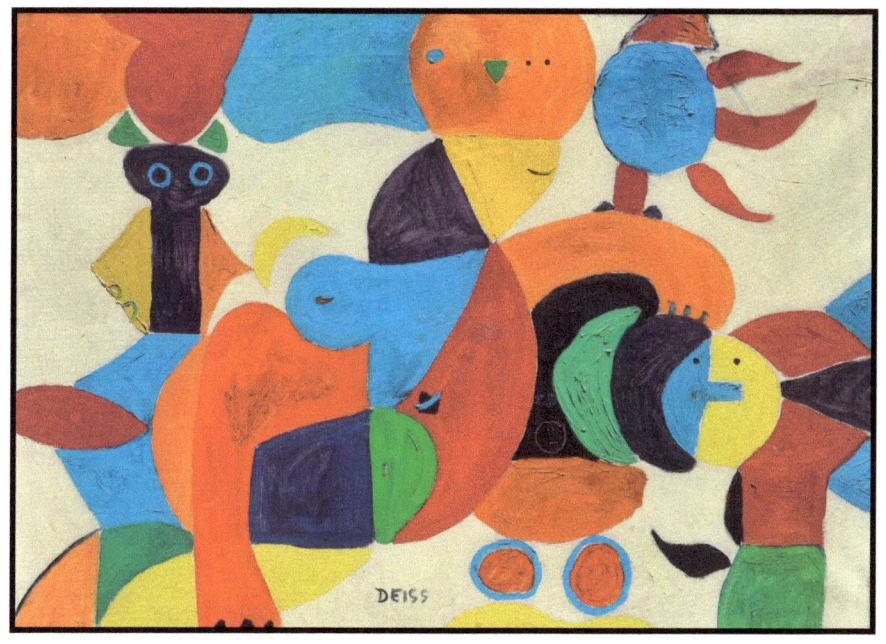

Satyr with Nursemaid

Luckily my brother's fears didn't last. He grew into an uninhibited, free spirit.

When Casio and I were a little older, our family moved to Wellfleet, in Massachusetts. My brother sailed in Cape Cod Bay, learning to recognize the moods of the winds and currents. He spent many hours sanding the bottom of his wooden cat boat, so that when he was racing it would glide through the waves as smoothly as glass.

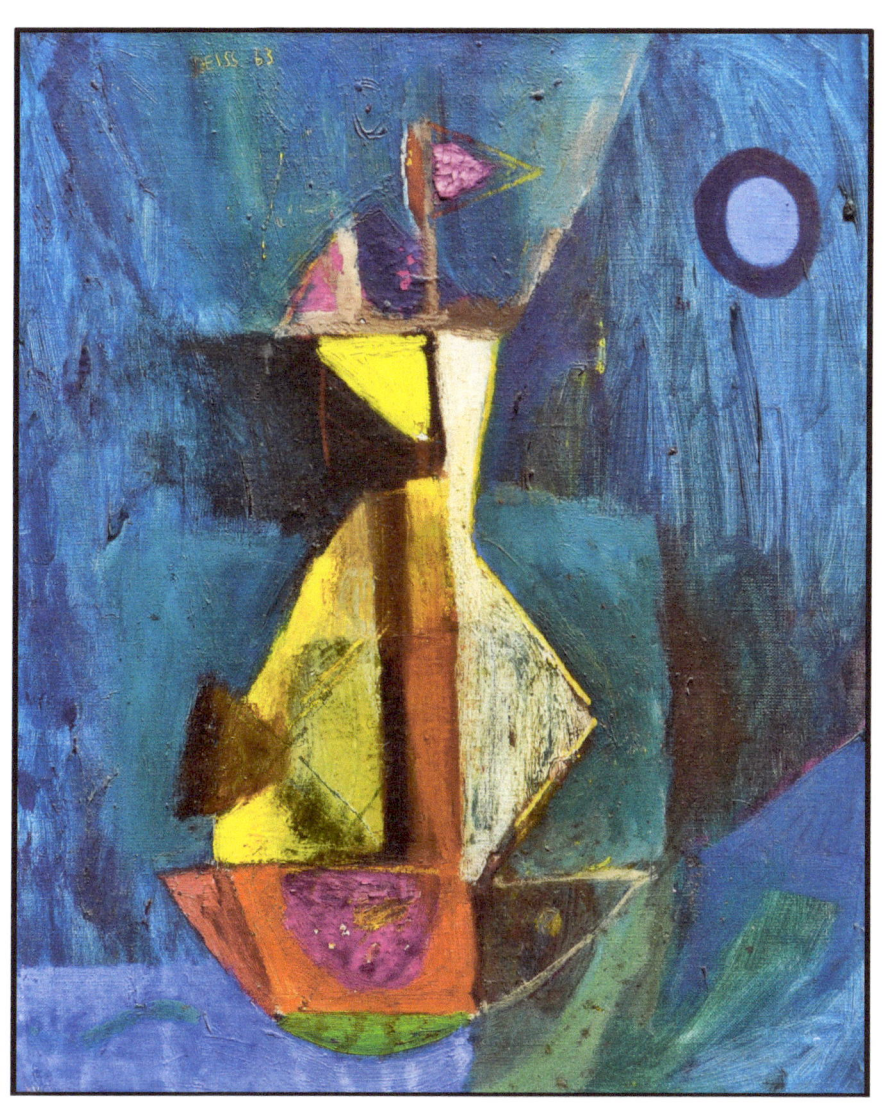

Boat with Blue Moon

At one time, I believed that my brother and I would be friends all our lives, sitting together in old age in rocking chairs on the porch, looking out over the pond below our family home and reminiscing about the past, our shared memories.

But in 1955 we moved to Rome, and from then on we lived back and forth between Wellfleet and Italy, mostly based at our villa in Positano. The path of our lives was totally changed, sorrows and joys intermingled in a multi-faceted existence, our kaleidoscopic vision of life constantly changing.

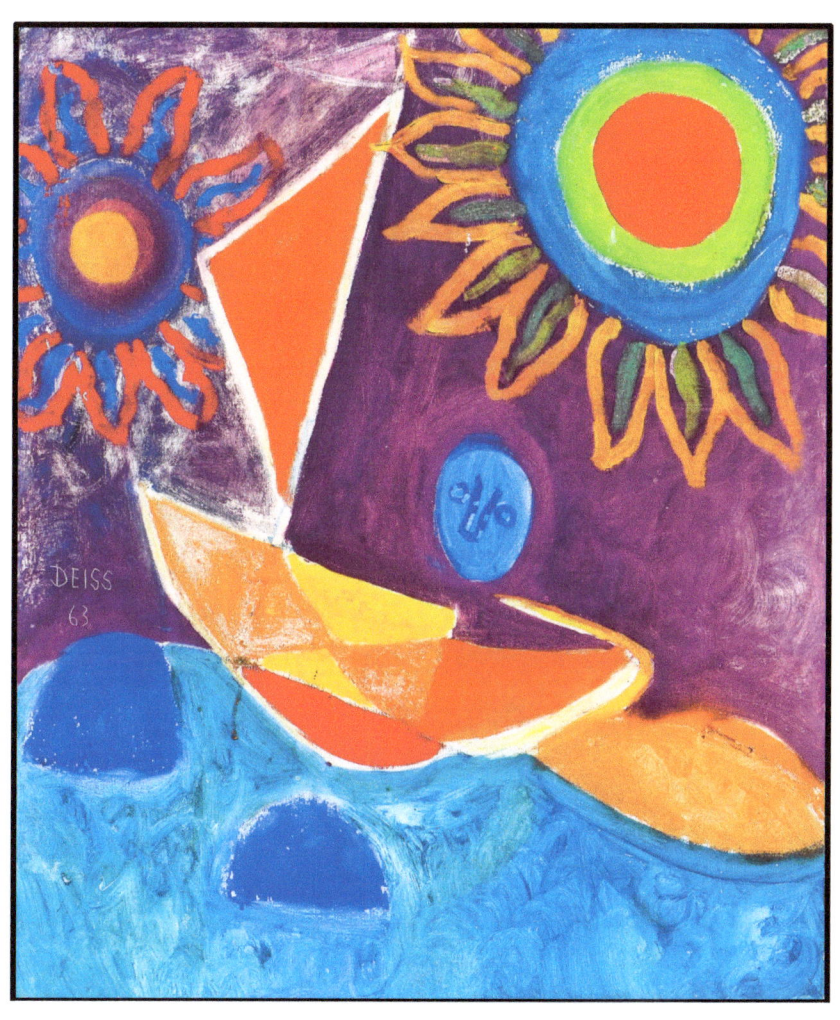

Sailboat with Giant Sun

It was in Positano that Casio learned to leap off the cliffs and dive deep down into the Mediterranean Sea. Lace-like foam spread out as he sliced through the emerald-blue water, disappearing below the surface.

Living in Positano was like being inside a flower-filled cistern, in a village of extraordinary beauty, remote from the real world but filled with, in addition to the local people, artists, writers, photographers, dancers, choreographers, actors and film-makers.

When I grew up, I wanted to climb out into the flat land above, to explore the world that most people inhabit. What a mistake that was! Once out of Paradise, you can never go back. We never again found any place like it.

Sometimes I have imagined that we are all still there, my family and our animals, our friends, living in another dimension... that Casio and I are both inside that magical cistern, forever young.

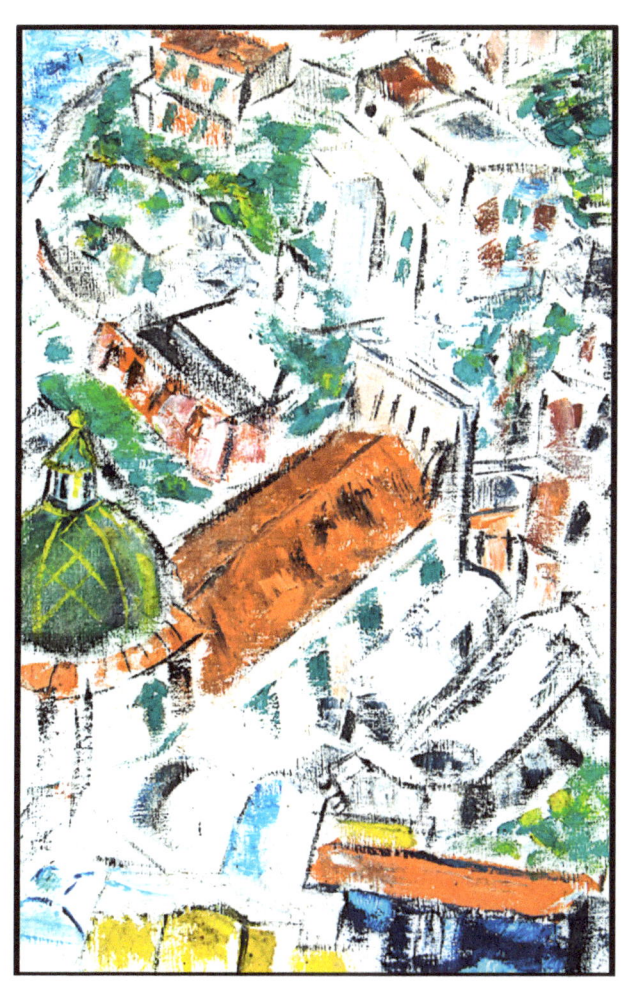

Chiesa di Santa Maria Assunta

The terraced gardens of our villa had lemon and orange trees, date palms, walnut and almond trees, as well as peach and apricot trees. In the fall, figs on the tree outside my bedroom window dripped honey, and bright orange persimmons hung ripe from barren branches.

A seashell fountain was set into the wall next to a glass-topped table on the terrace nearest the kitchen. Father always turned it on when guests were coming. Our black cat, Asfaltino, amused himself by dropping down from the wisteria covered arbor that shaded the table onto unsuspecting guests.

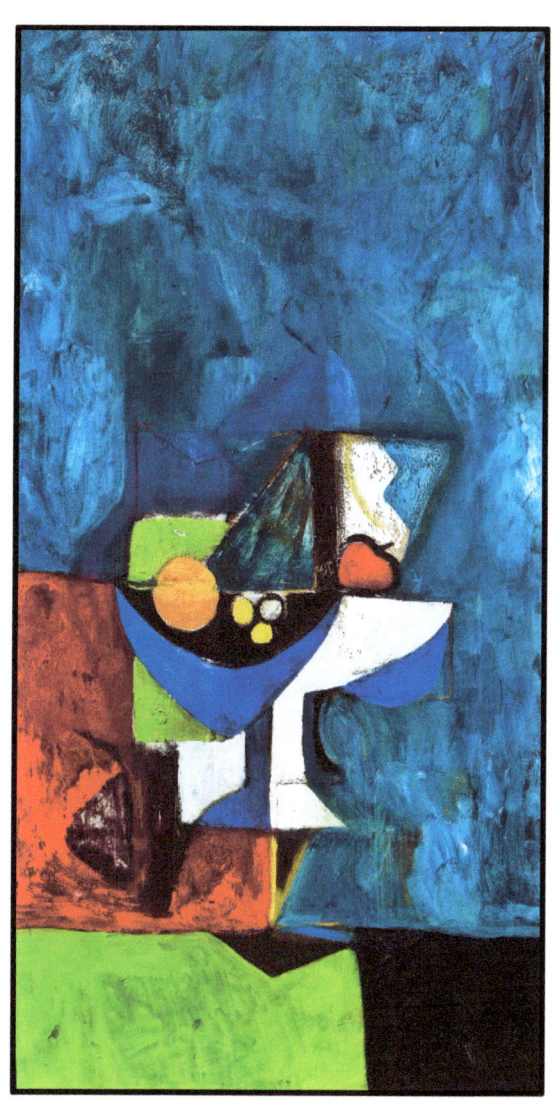

Still Life - Fruit

At night, the lanterns on the fishing boats glimmered across the water. The fishermen leaned on their oars as they rowed out to sea and cast their nets, just as their forefathers had done for generations before them, back to ancient Roman times.

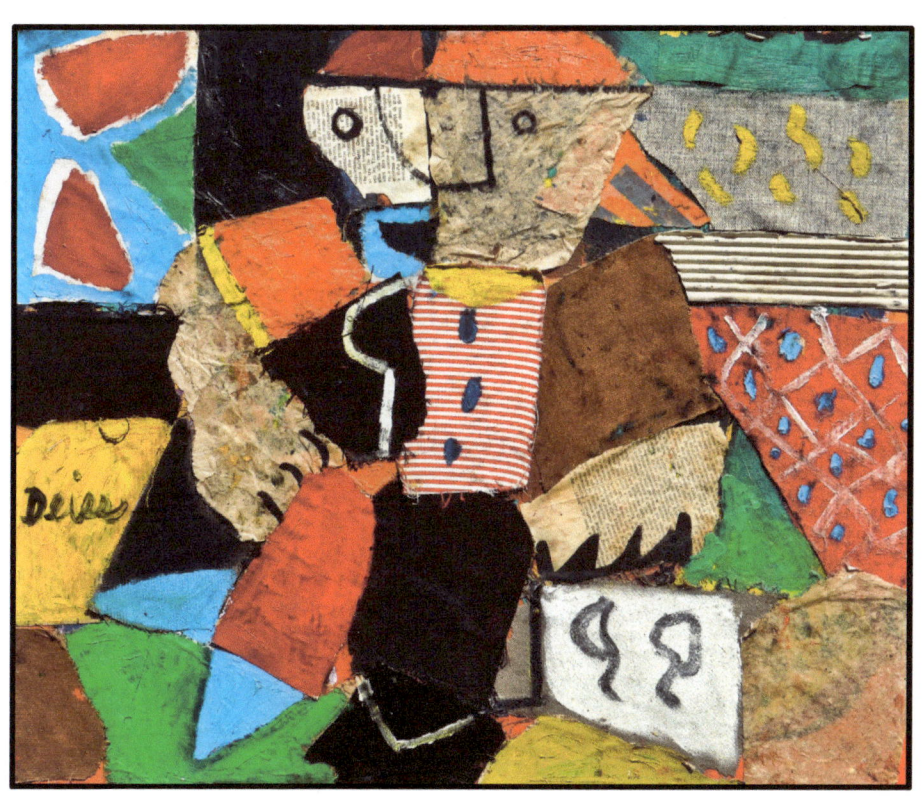

Fisherman on the Beach

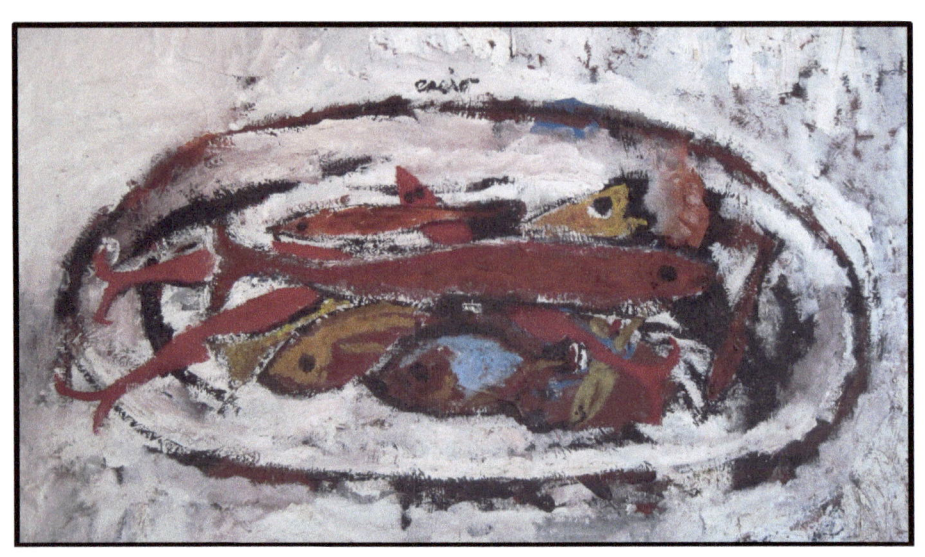

Platter of Fish

Mother, listening to opera and sipping white wine, sometimes prepared fish in the Sicilian way, stuffed with rosemary, bread crumbs, pine nuts and raisins. She baked them in the wood-fired oven and served them with Lacryma Christi, a wine made from grapes grown on the slopes of Mount Vesuvius.

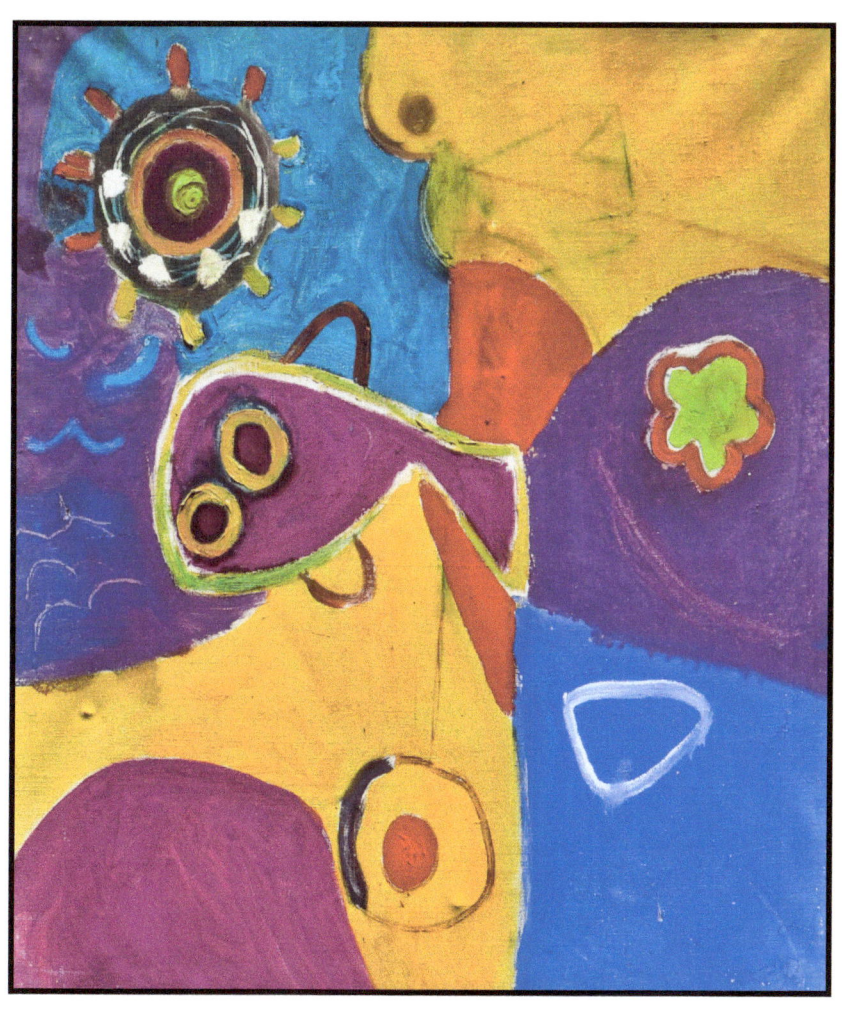

Leaping Fish

When we were children, we had a costume box filled with clothes from a bygone era. Among other treasures, our great-aunt Alice had given us velvet breeches, her organdie wedding dress with room for a bustle, with tiny buttons down the back that needed a ladies' maid to fasten them, a bull whip from India that had belonged to her husband, and a silk parasol with an intricately caved ivory handle. We spent many hours dressing up, imagining ourselves in another place and time, play-acting.

Years later, we lived in Fiesole. Looking past a nunnery down the valley, you could see the rooftops of Florence, where Casio attended the Accademia di Belle Arti di Firenze. Fascinated by the Renaissance clothing in many of the paintings he studied, he began painting costumes in his own style, and wearing elegant embroidered clothing.

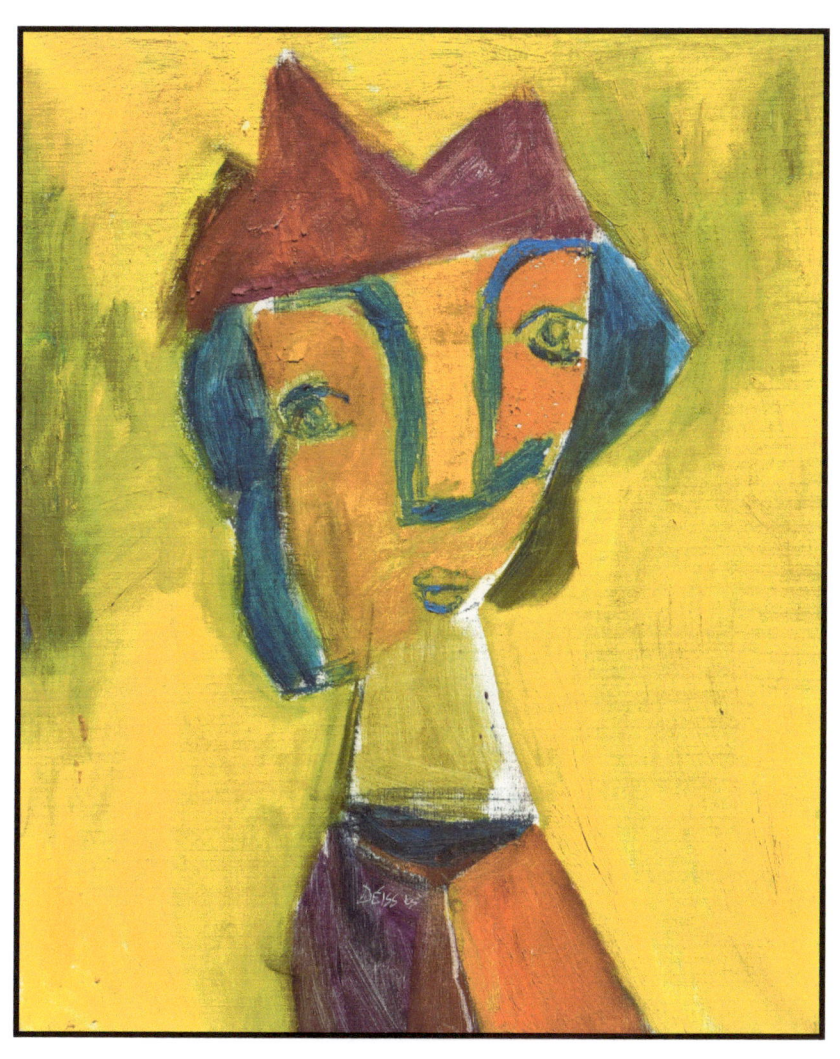

Woman in a Red Hat

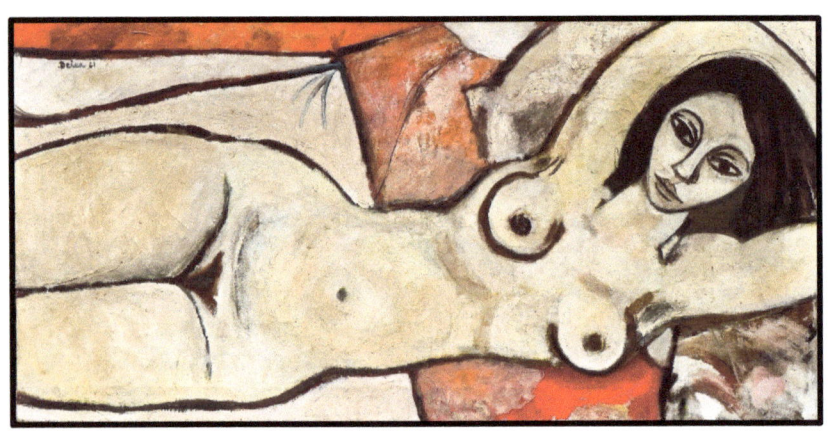

Reclining Nude

Casio liked to paint and draw his friends. Many people relied on him. He was a beacon for unhappy, lost souls who found solace in his presence.

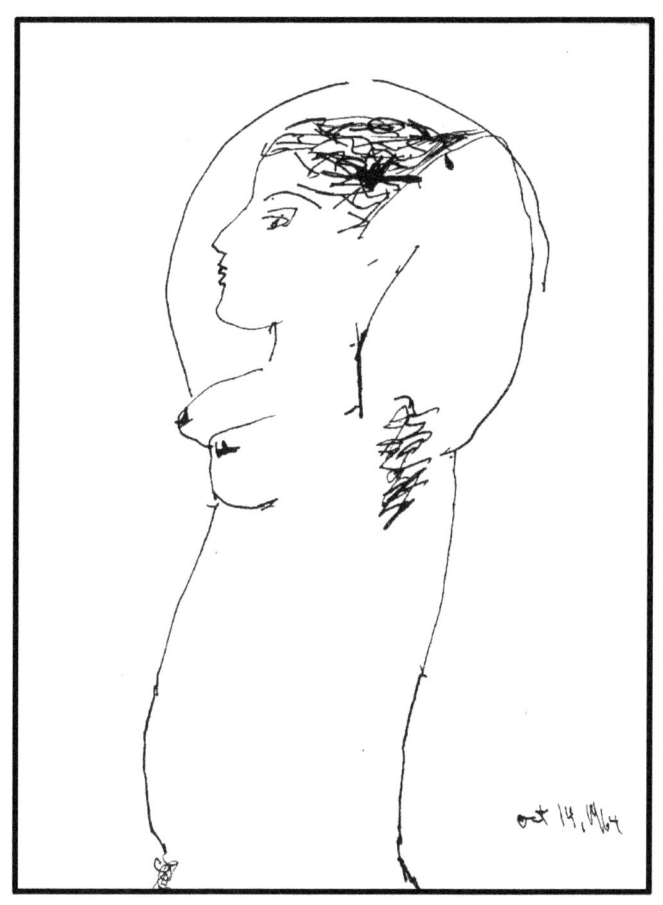

Ellen

Casio made fun of everything, even himself, smiling innocently, a dimple showing in his cheek. He never had respect for authority, right from the very beginning. Moments after he was born, he peed in the nurse's eye. Later the Parents joked about it. They felt it was prophetic.

He lampooned the authorities, especially politicians. In restaurants, we watched porcine Christian Democrats, members of a conservative political party powerful at the time, gorging themselves on song birds skewered through their plucked bodies. They popped the little birds whole, heads and all, into their gaping mouths.

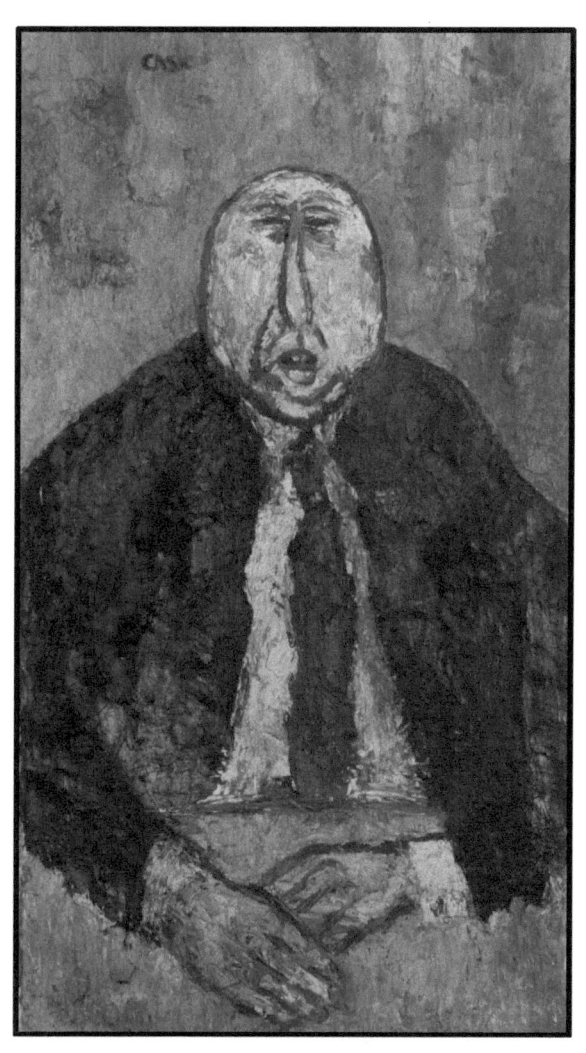

Christian Democrat

... and even the Church did not go unscathed.

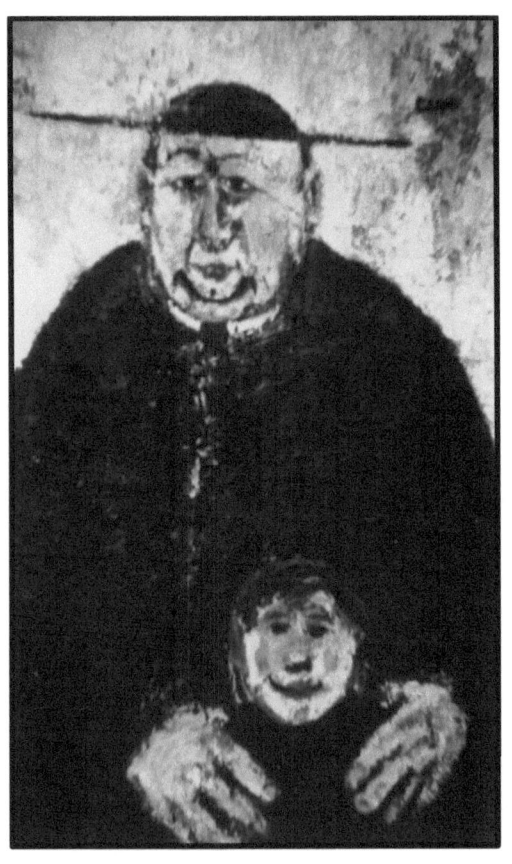

Priest with Choir Boy

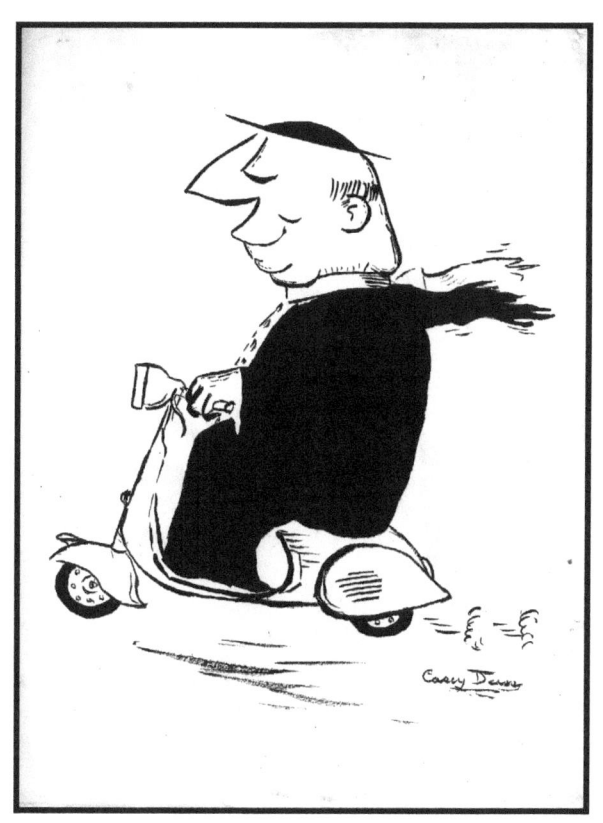

Priest on a Motor Scooter

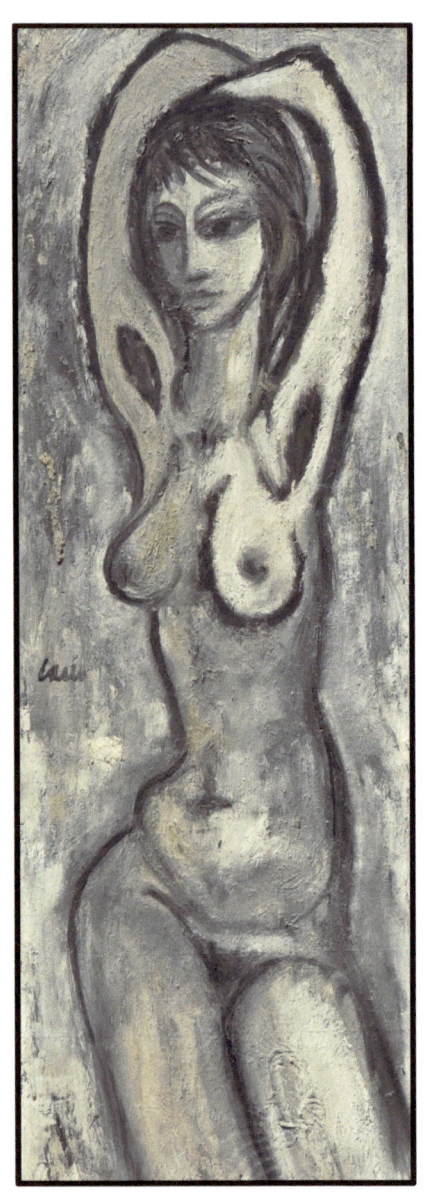

Elena

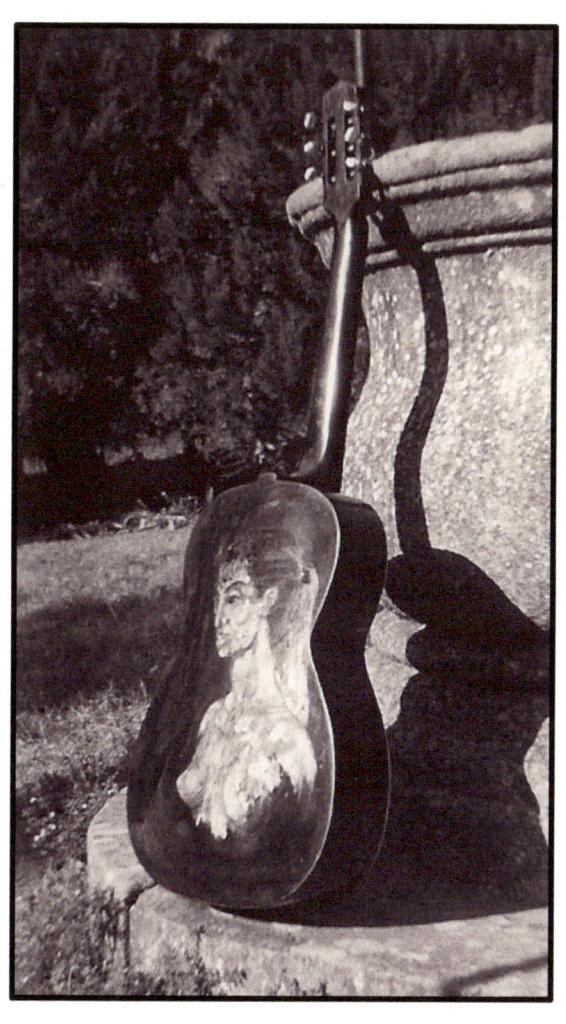

Painted Guitar

Most days Casio played his guitar for hours... Bach, Albinoni, Vivaldi, Marcello... the notes seemed to hang in the air long after he ceased playing.

Casio had a Martin guitar. One day when he was hanging out in Washington Square in New York, he met a tramp. After the tramp played the fabulous guitar, Casio gave it to him. He said the man was an incredible musician and should have the guitar.

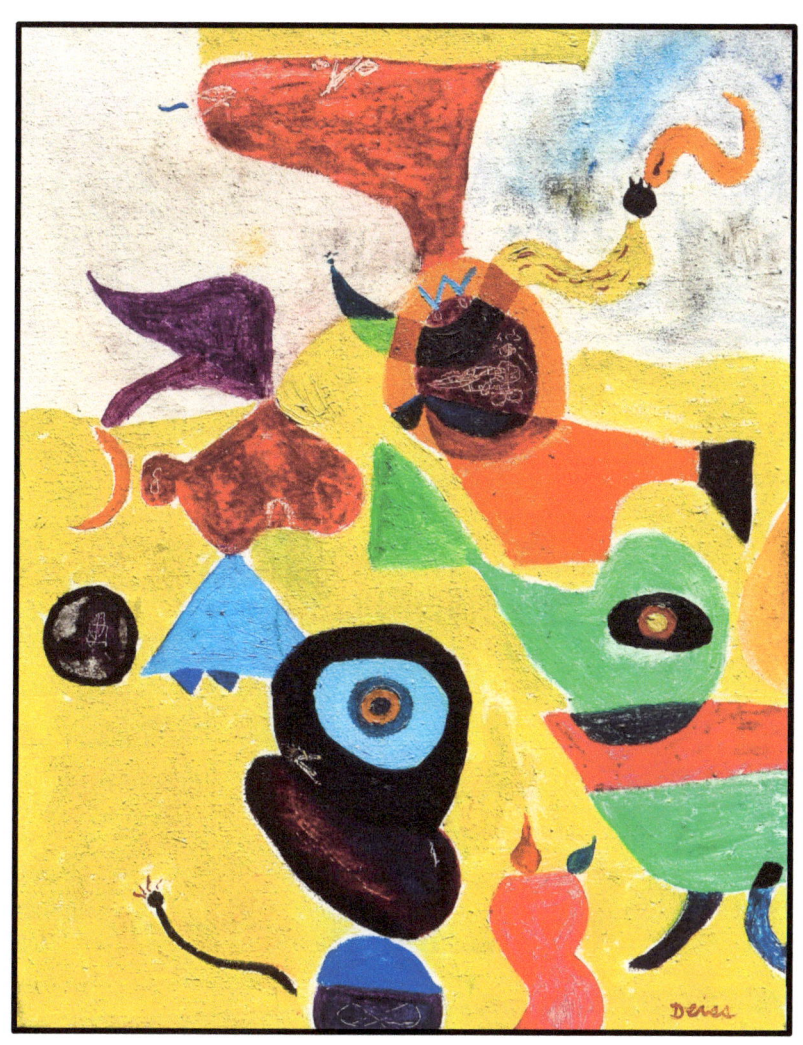

Musicians

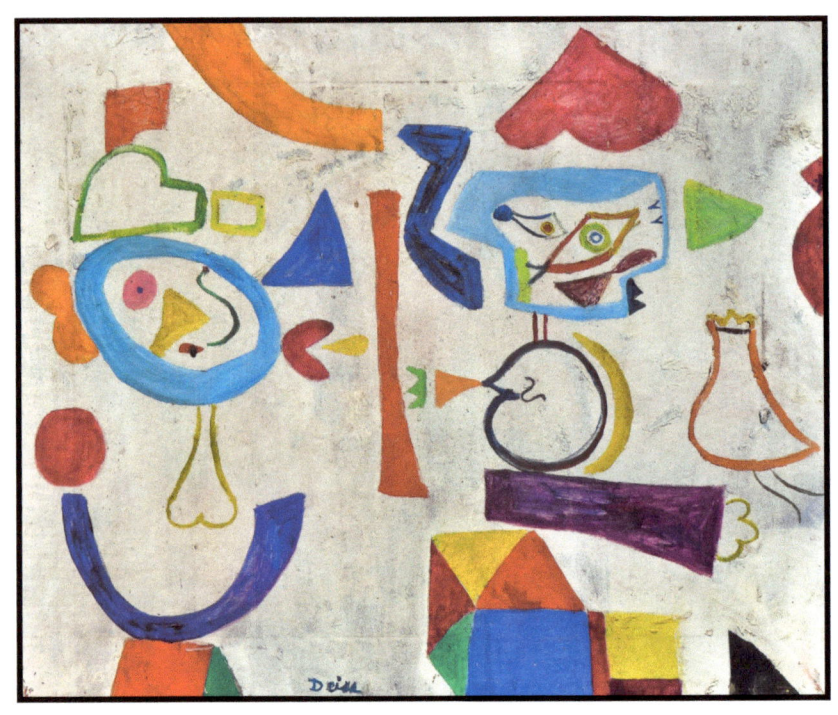

Whirling Dancers

Casio loved to dance, and never lacked for partners.

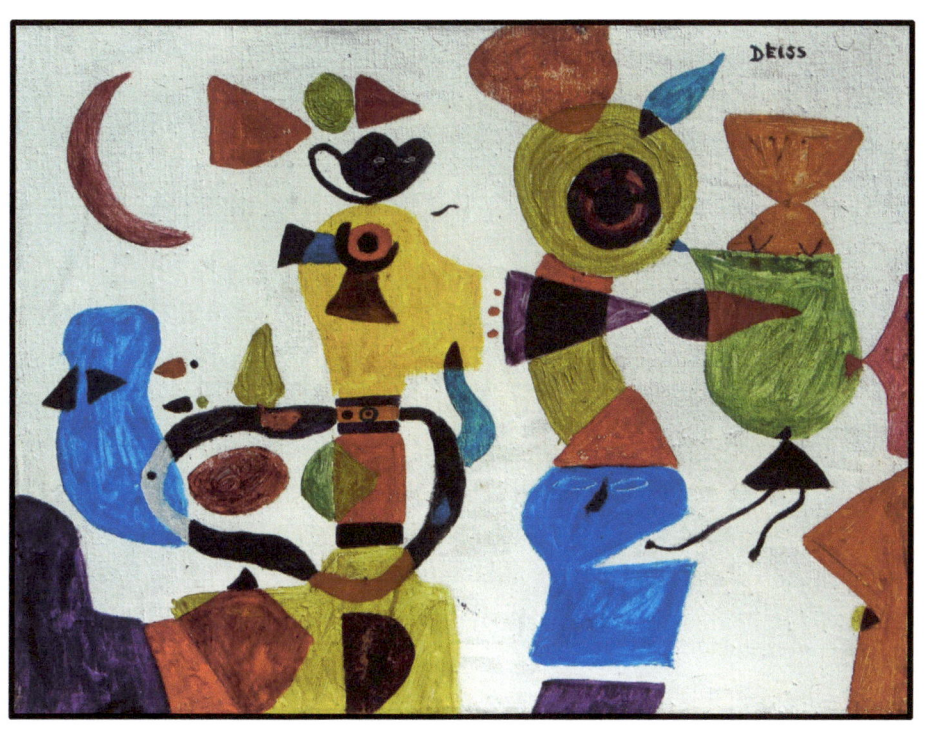

La Gioia! Happiness!

Casio shared his sensitivity and appreciation of beauty with others, bringing great joy into all our lives.

In the fall of 1969, Casio and his wife Diana were living in a farmhouse on a hilltop in the countryside not far from Rome, near Lake Bracciano. They were waiting for the birth of their second child, having lost a baby girl the previous year.

September 6 was a raw, cold day, and it was raining. The only heat was from the large open fireplace, where the cats, dogs and chickens had gathered round the fire, which had burned down to embers. Casio picked up his machete and went outside to get some wood for the fire. A brilliant flash of lightning was followed by a deafening crack of thunder... and Casio lay crumpled on the stone steps that ran down along the side of the building.

A little over a month later his daughter I-la Casy was born, lessening our burden of grief after he left us forever for his own fanciful Garden of Eden.

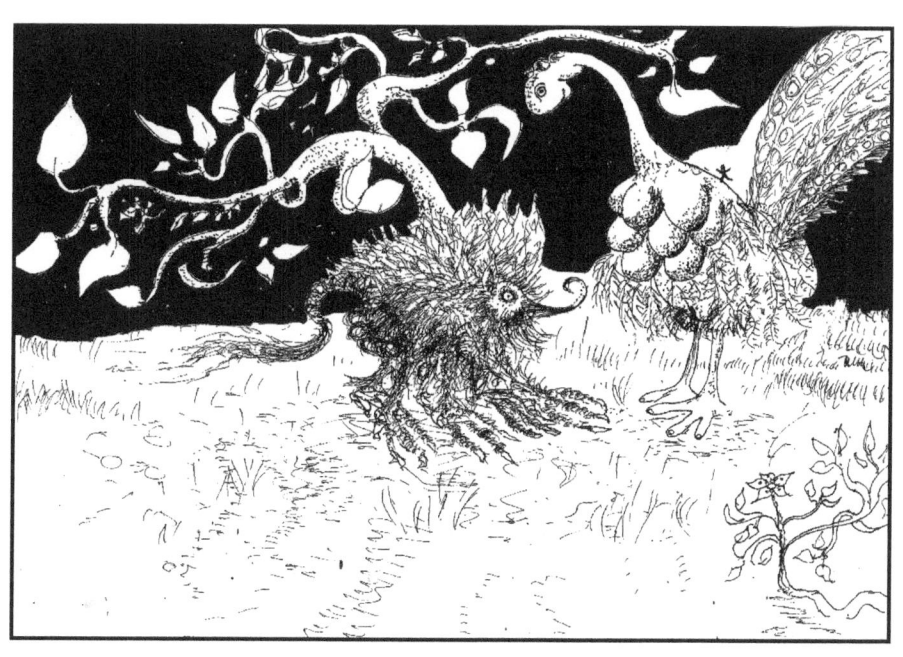

The Garden of Eden

Illustrations

Cover and frontispiece: Portrait of John Casy Deiss (Photo by Mimmo Maccioni)

Monsters, 1961. (Sketch) From letter to J. Springer

Self-Portrait (Sketch). Deiss Trust

Tummy Touching, ca. 1963. Deiss Trust

Satyr with Nursemaid, 1964. Deiss Trust

Boat with Blue Moon, 1963. Deiss Trust

Sailboat with Giant Sun, 1963. Deiss Trust

Chiesa di Santa Maria Assunta, ca. 1960. Deiss Trust

Still Life - Fruit, 1963. Deiss Trust

Fisherman on the Beach (Collage), 1964. Deiss Trust

Platter of Fish, ca. 1963. Deiss Trust

Leaping Fish, ca. 1963. Deiss Trust

Woman in a Red Hat, 1963. Deiss Trust

Reclining Nude, 1961. Deiss Trust

Ellen, 1964 (Sketch). E. Delbanco Collection

Christian Democrat, 1964. R. Bueno Collection

Priest on a Motor Scooter (Sketch). Deiss Trust

Priest with Choir Boy, ca. 1964. (Snapshot photo of painting, owned by P. Barkentin)

Elena, 1960. H. B. Jarvenpa Collection

Painted Guitar. (Snapshot photo, owner unknown)

Musicians, 1964. Deiss Trust

Whirling Dancers, 1964. Deiss Trust

La Gioia! Happiness!, 1964. N. C. Menendez Collection

The Garden of Eden, 1966 (Sketch) Deiss Trust

Photo credits: Photos of artwork courtesy of Judah Chivian.

Author's note: Due to space considerations, images of Casio's ceramic work and some paintings from the Deiss Trust and other collections have not been included in this memoir, and some paintings are lost.

www.ingramcontent.com/pod-product-compliance
Lightning Source LLC
Chambersburg PA
CBHW041943240526
45473CB00033B/489